# 24 EASY CLASSICAL SOLOS

## PIANO ACCOMPANIMENT

*VIOLIN • VIOLA • CELLO • BASS*

BOOK 1

## HARRY HUNT, JR., MFA

24 Easy Classical Solos Piano Accompaniment - Violin, Viola, Cello, Bass: Book 1
Harry Hunt, Jr., MFA

©2024 Harry Hunt, Jr.

All Rights Reserved. No part of this book may be reproduced in any form without written permission from the publisher.

Published by A2G Entertainment Inc.
Chicago, IL
harryhuntjr.com

ISBN: 978-1-954127-31-9 (Paperback)

Printed in the USA
Second Edition

## CONTENTS

1. Hot Cross Buns  1
2. Lightly Row  2
3. Lullaby  3
4. Au Clair De La Lune  4
5. Twinkle  6
6. Scarborough Fair  7
7. Oh Susanna  8
8. Marriage Of Figaro  10
9. Long Long Ago  11
10. Rondeau  12
11. Piano Concerto #3  14
12. Symphony #7 (2nd Movement)  16
13. German Dance  18
14. Choral Fantasy  19
15. The Heavens Are Telling  20
16. Bourrée (Water Music)  22
17. Carnival Of Venice  24
18. Sonatina #1  26
19. Londonderry Air  28
20. Blue Danube  30
21. Minuet I  32
22. Eine Kleine  34
23. Symphony #7 (3rd Movement)  36
24. Minuet  38
  42

# 1. HOT CROSS BUNS

©2024 Harry Hunt, Jr.

# 2. LIGHTLY ROW

©2024 Harry Hunt, Jr.

# 3. LULLABY

Brahms

©2024 Harry Hunt, Jr.

# 4. AU CLAIR DE LA LUNE

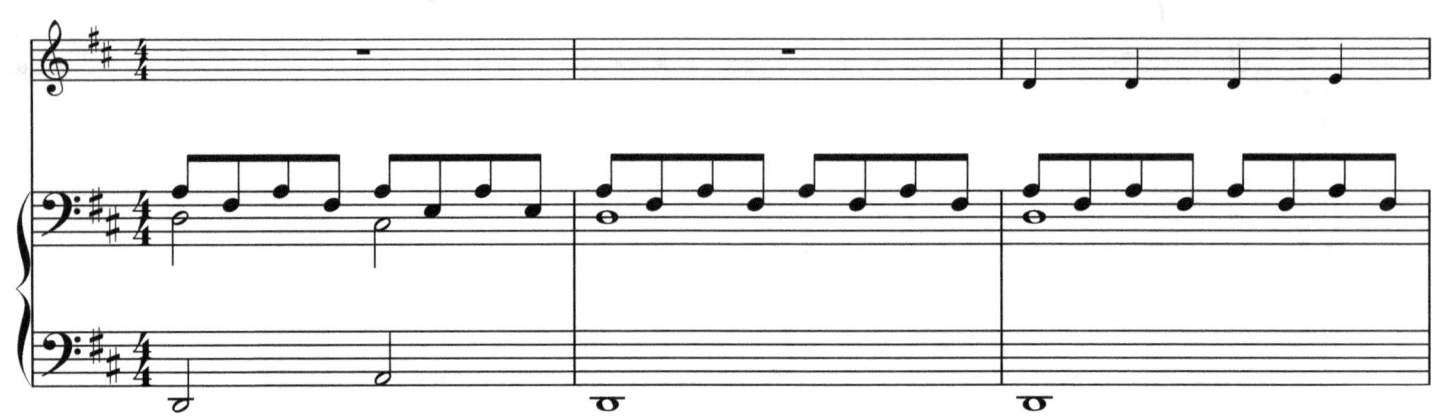

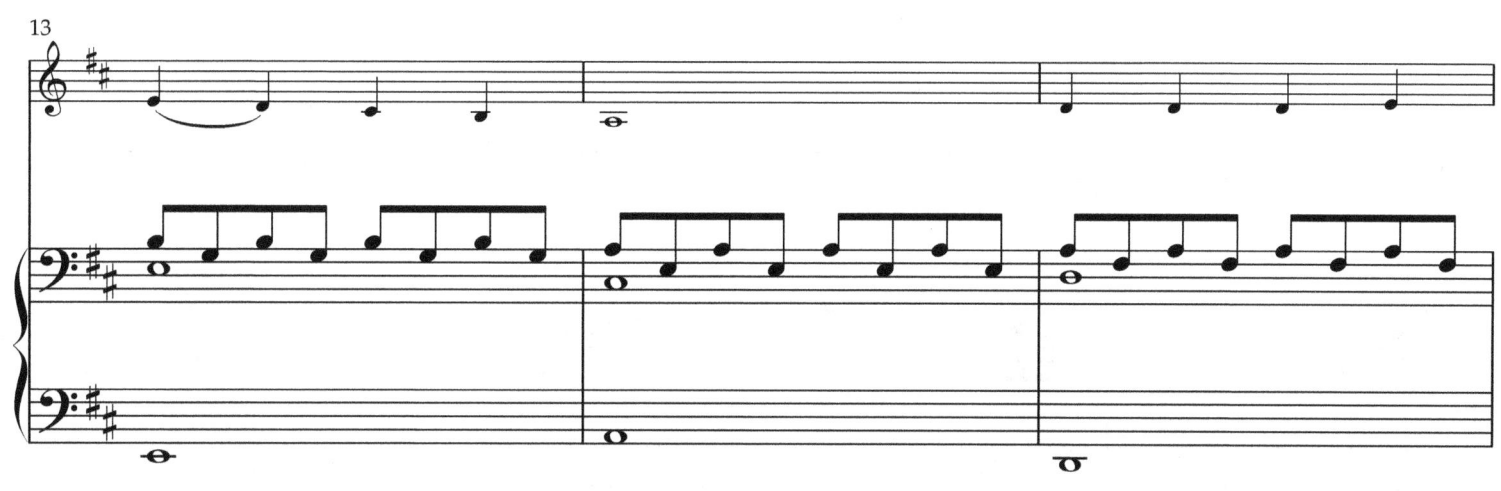

©2024 Harry Hunt, Jr.

# 5. TWINKLE

©2024 Harry Hunt, Jr.

# 6. SCARBOROUGH FAIR

©2024 Harry Hunt, Jr.

# 7. OH SUSANNA

Foster

# 8. MARRIAGE OF FIGARO

Mozart

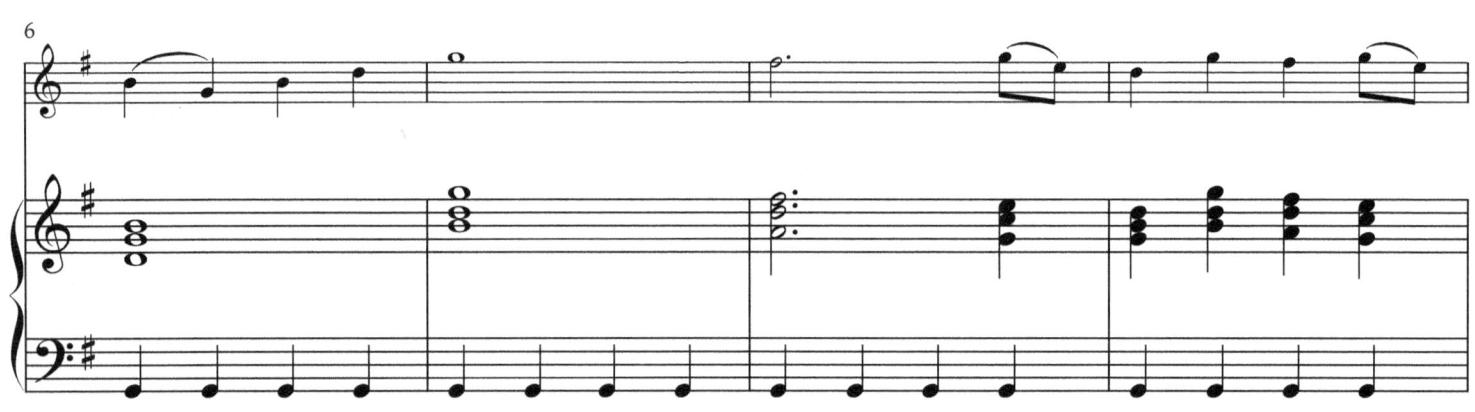

10 ©2024 Harry Hunt, Jr.

# 9. LONG LONG AGO

Bayly

# 10. RONDEAU

Mouret

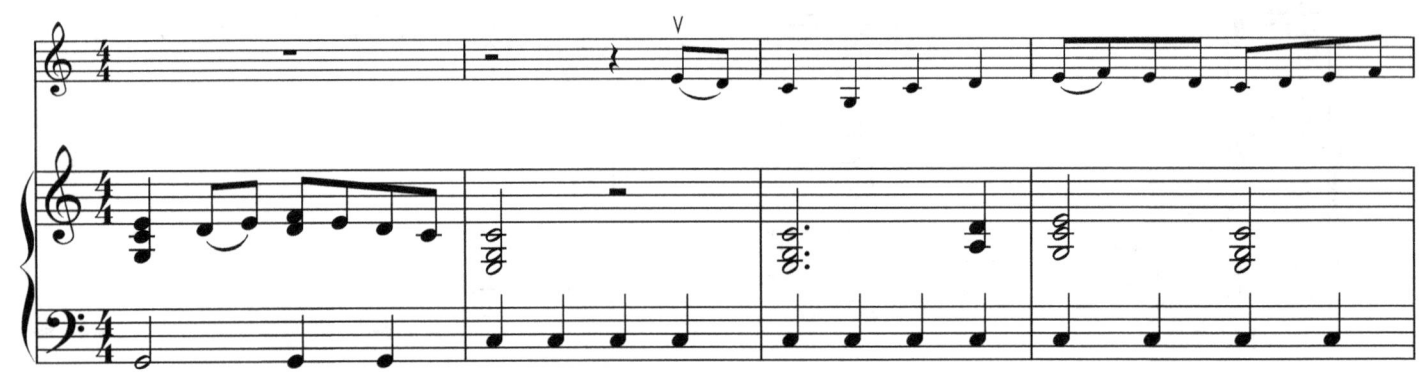

# 11. PIANO CONCERTO #3

Beethoven

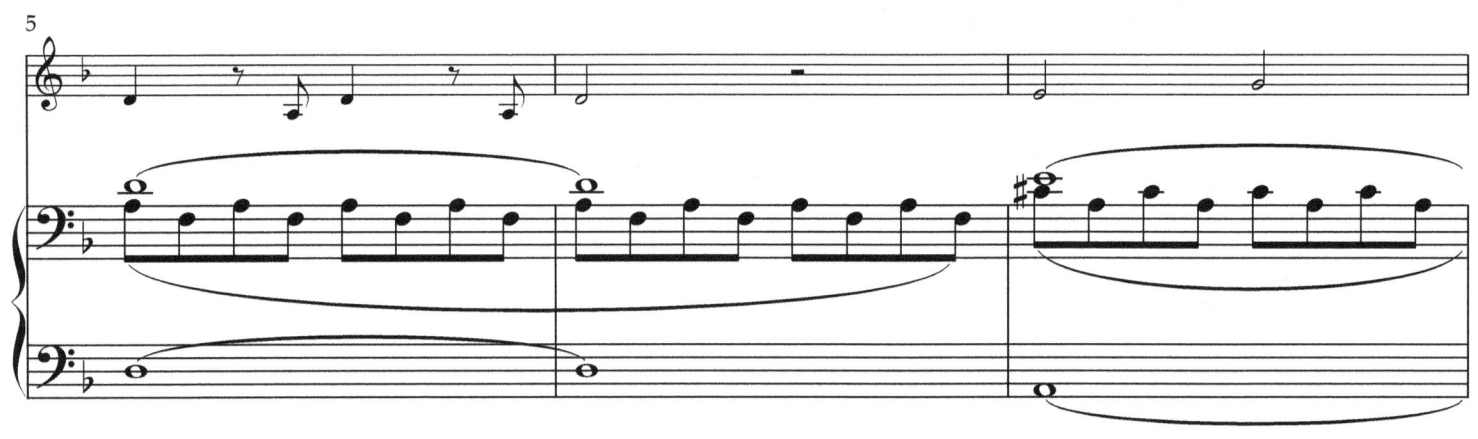

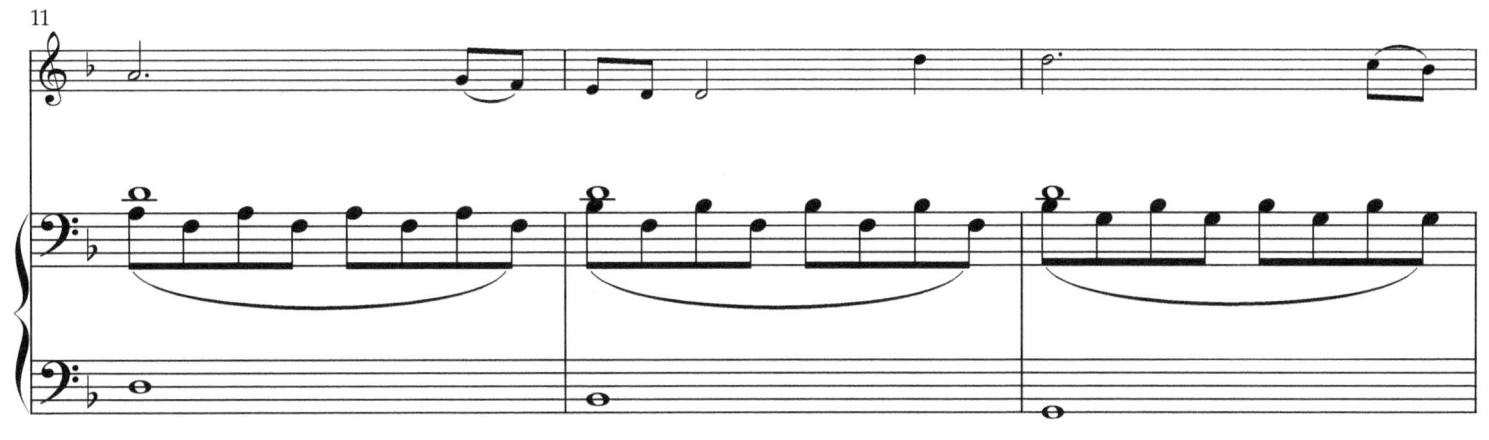
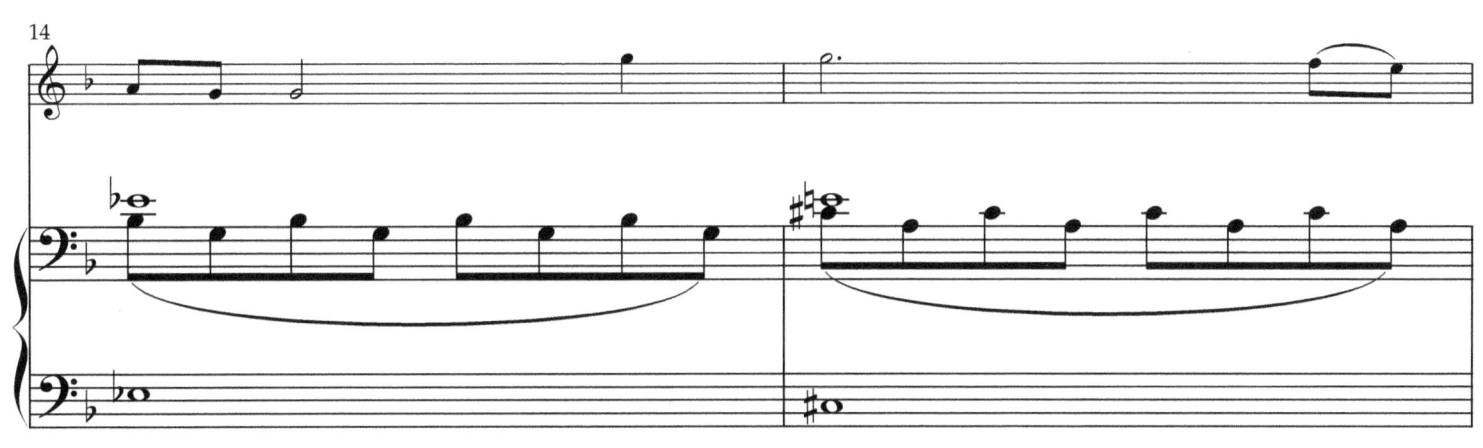

# 12. SYMPHONY #7 (2nd Movement)

Beethoven

# 13. GERMAN DANCE

Mozart

# 14. CHORAL FANTASY

Beethoven

©2024 Harry Hunt, Jr.

# 15. THE HEAVENS ARE TELLING

Haydn

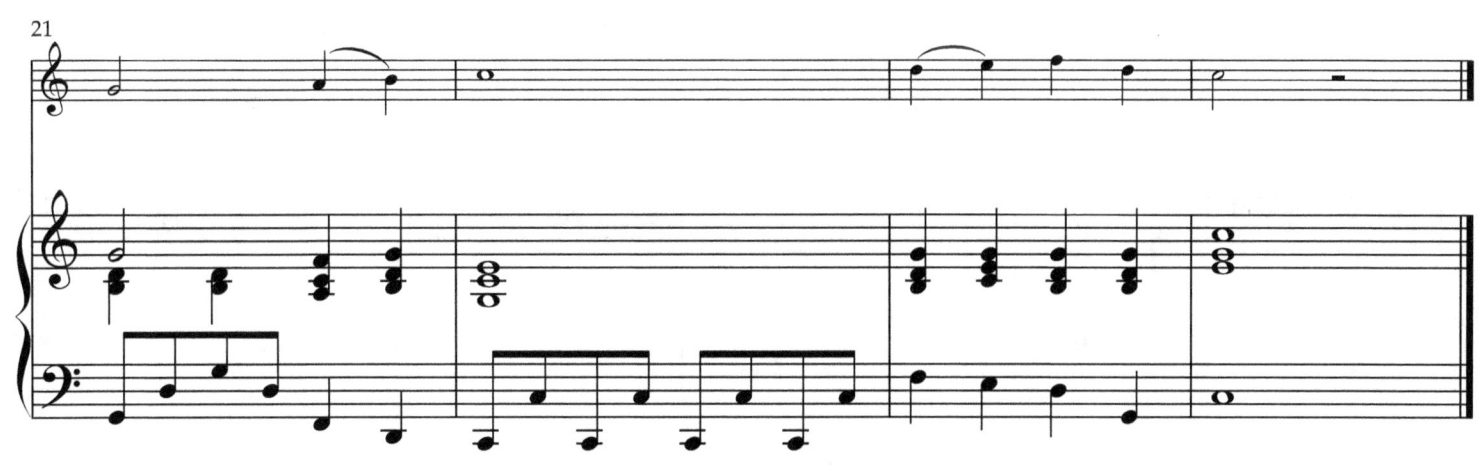

# 16. BOURRÉE (Water Music)

Handel

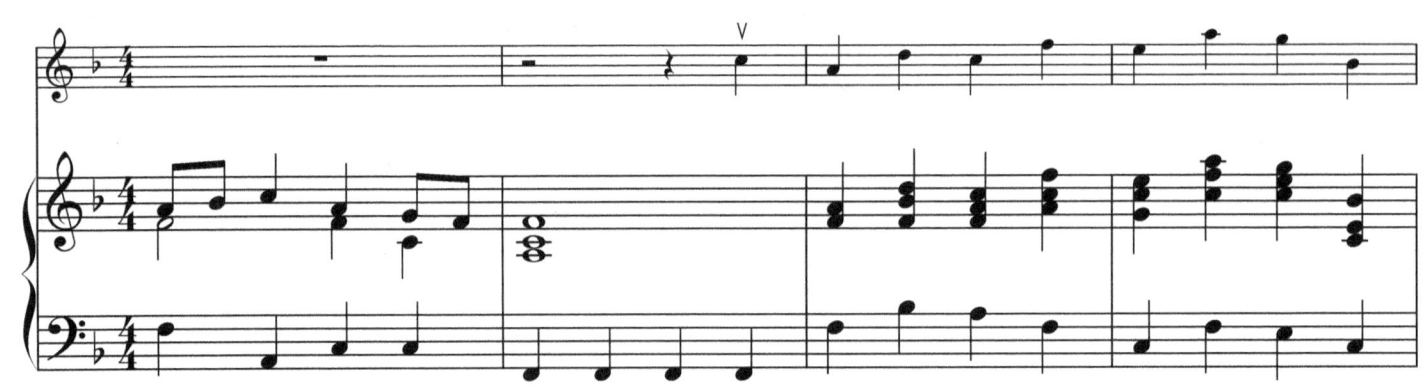

©2024 Harry Hunt, Jr.

# 17. CARNIVAL OF VENICE

Benedict

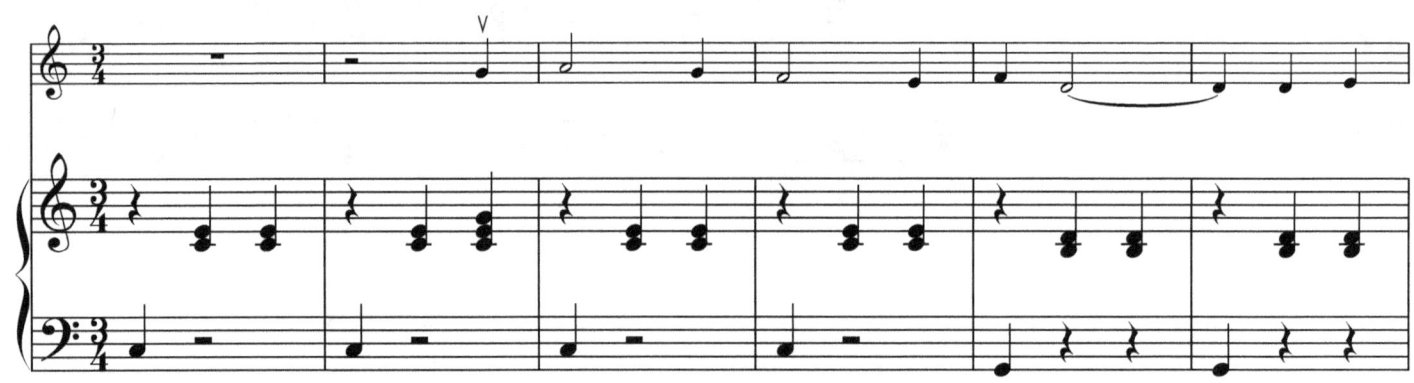

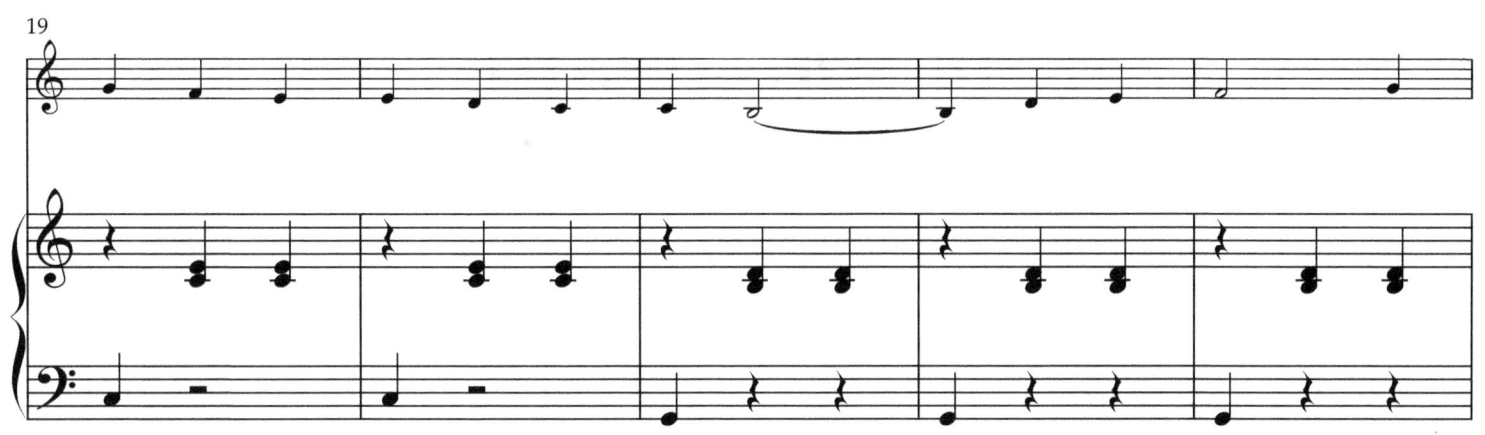

# 18. SONATINA #1

Beethoven

# 19. LONDONDERRY AIR

# 20. BLUE DANUBE

Strauss

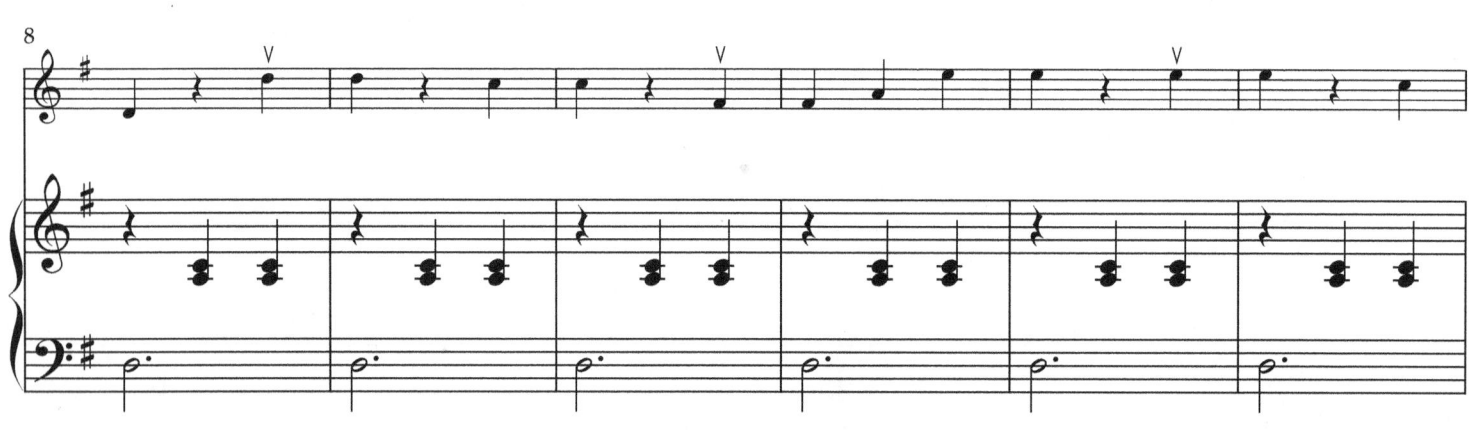
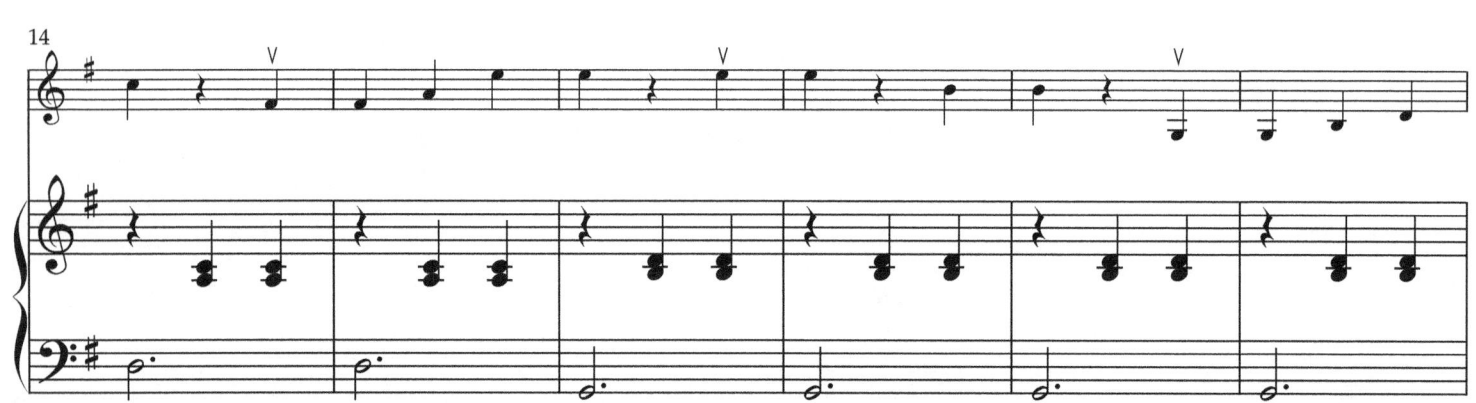

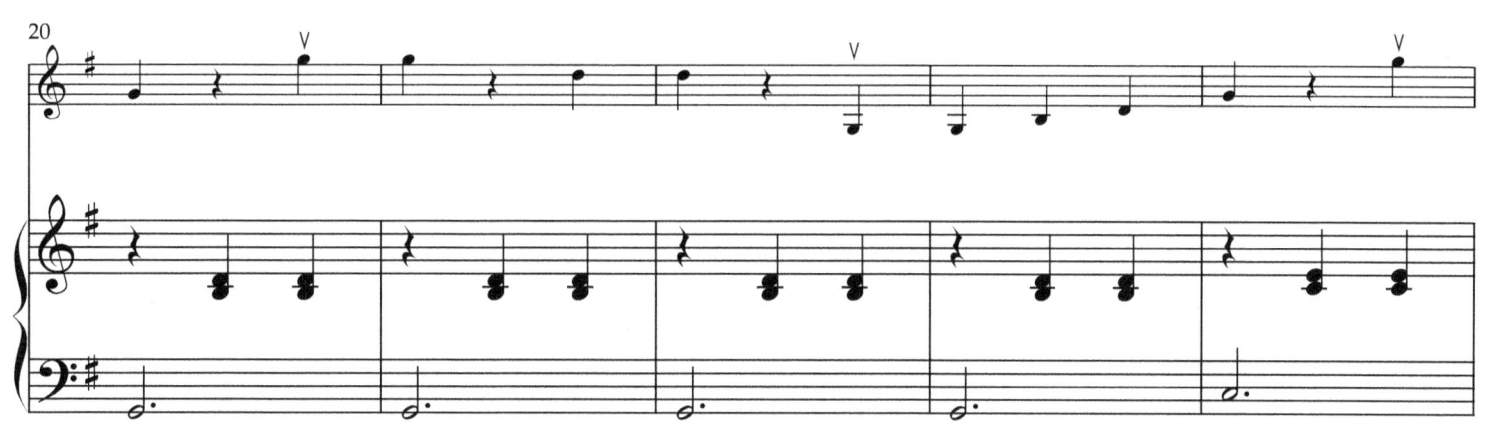
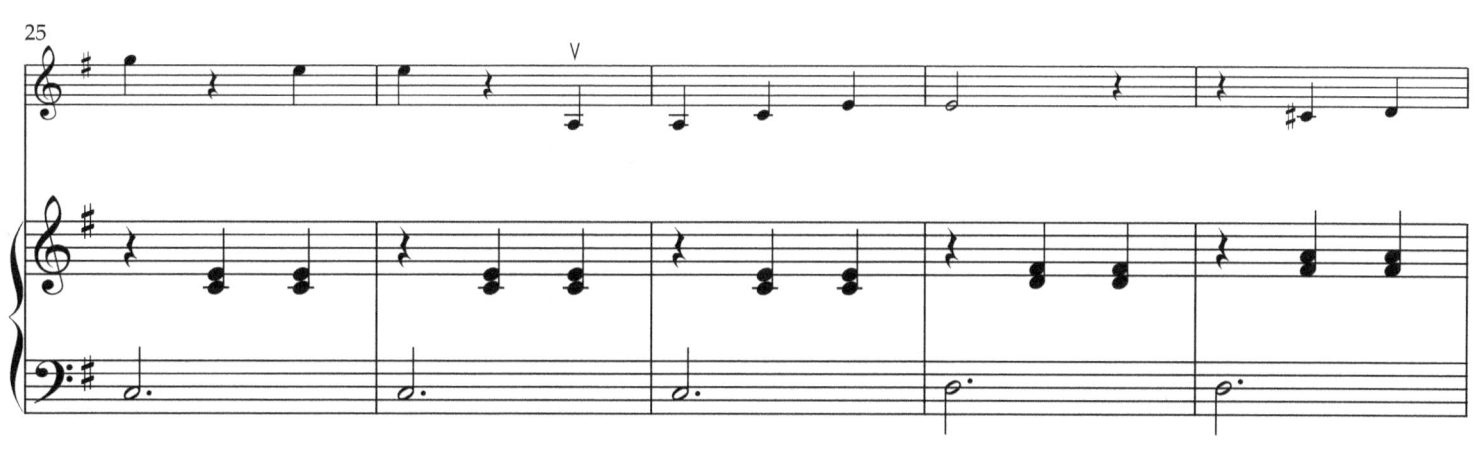
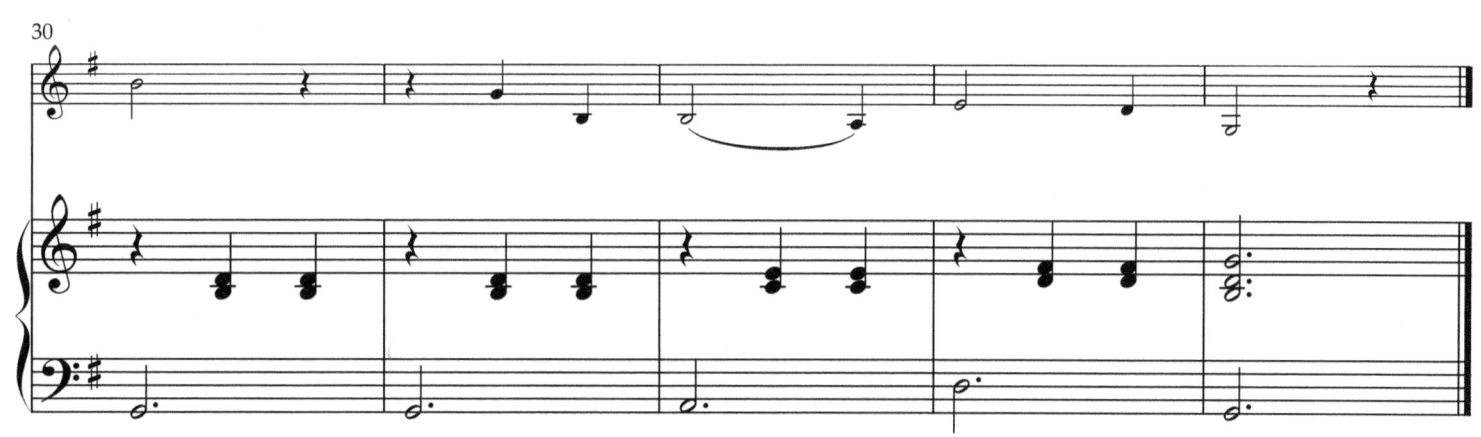

©2024 Harry Hunt, Jr.

# 21. MINUET I

Bach

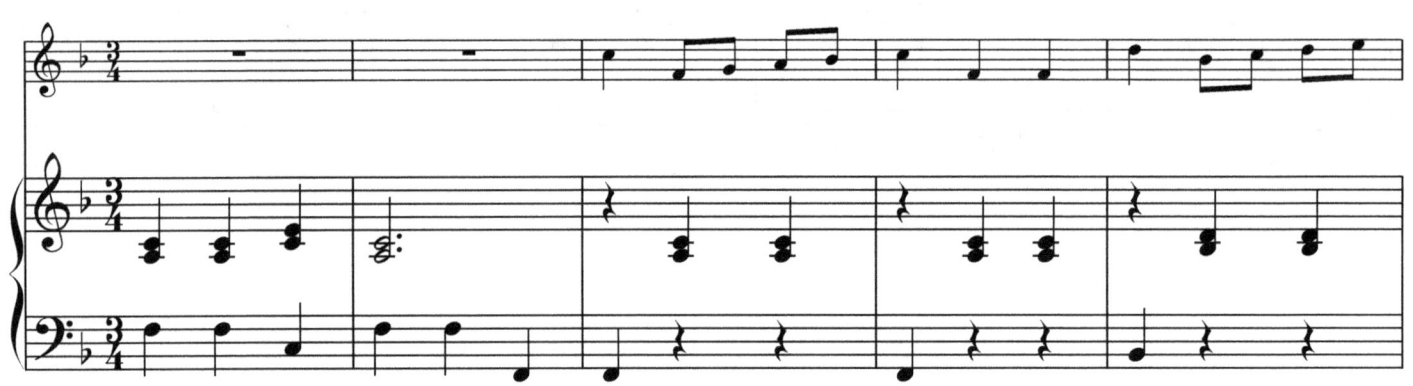

# 22. EINE KLEINE

Mozart

# 23. SYMPHONY #7 (3rd Movement)

Beethoven

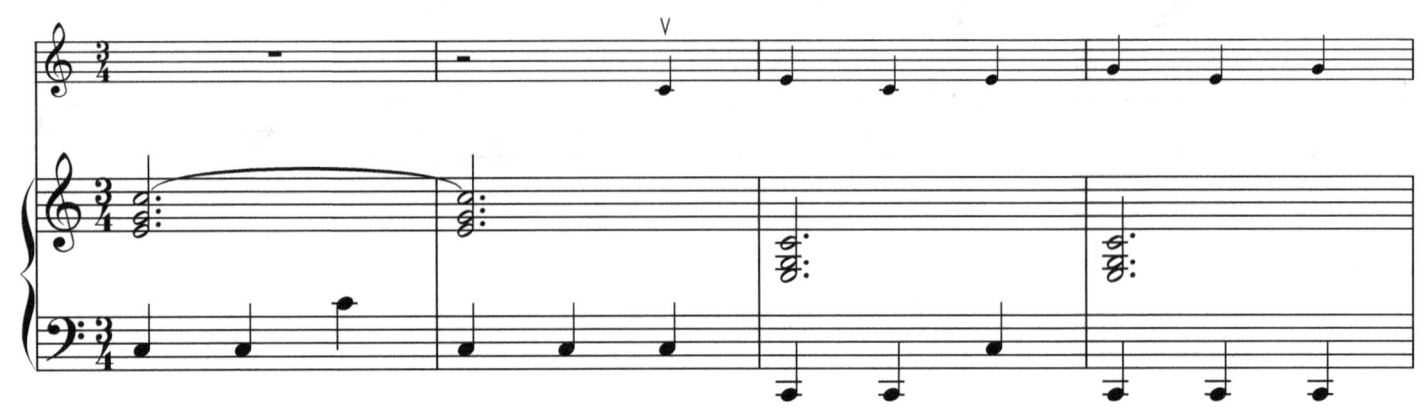

36  ©2024 Harry Hunt, Jr.

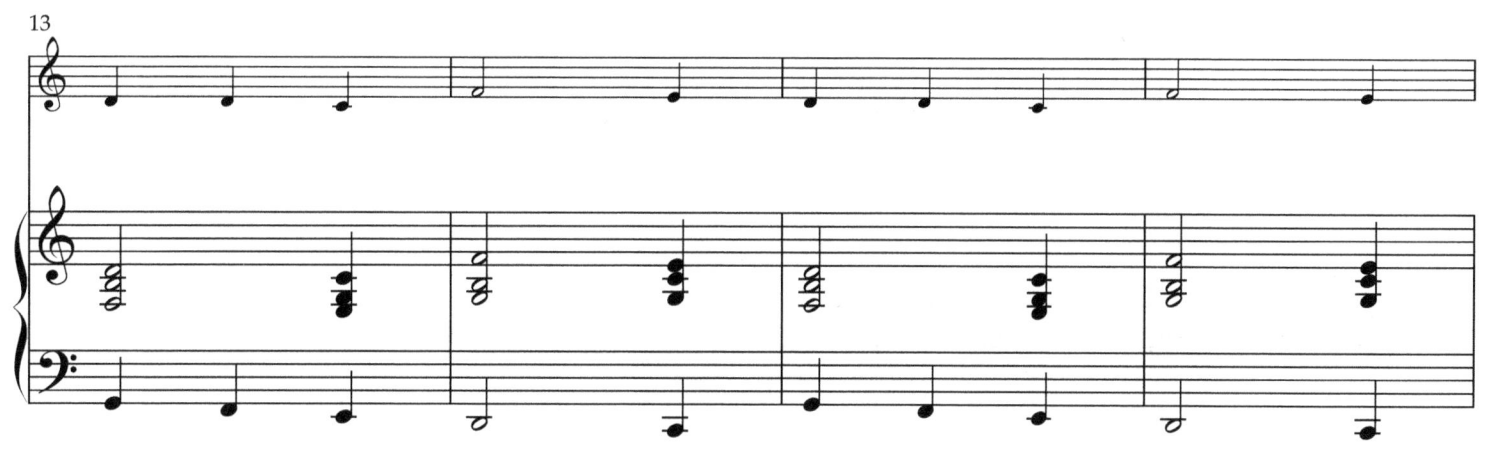

# 24. MINUET

Bach

www.ingramcontent.com/pod-product-compliance
Lightning Source LLC
Chambersburg PA
CBHW081351040426
42450CB00015B/3395